EL GRECO

THE VIRGIN   1583-85 Oil   *Private Collection, London*

EL GRECO

(Domenico Theotocopuli)

by

MAURICE LEGENDRE

Director of the Casa Velasquez, Madrid

THE HYPERION PRESS

AND

DUELL, SLOAN AND PEARCE

NEW YORK

THIS VOLUME
UNDER THE SUPERVISION OF
ANDRÉ GLOECKNER
WAS FIRST PUBLISHED MCMXLVII BY
THE HYPERION PRESS, NEW YORK.
THE TEXT WAS SET IN BASKERVILLE
BY ALFRED ROSSITER, INC., NEW
YORK; PHOTOGRAVURE ENGRAVED
AND PRINTED BY THE ULLMAN COM-
PANY, BROOKLYN, PAPER FROM THE
LINDE PAPER COMPANY, MASSACHU-
SETTS; COLOUR BLOCKS ENGRAVED
BY CLICHÉ UNION, PARIS; W. F. SEDG-
WICK, LTD., LONDON; THE BECK
ENGRAVING COMPANY, PHILADEL-
PHIA; AND THE CONDÉ NAST
ENGRAVERS, NEW YORK; LETTER-
PRESS PRINTING BY MARKETTE
PRINTING COMPANY, NEW YORK;
BINDING BY OSCAR POLOFSKY,
NEW YORK; JACKET DESIGNED BY
CLAUDE DE REMUSAT, PARIS.

PORTRAIT OF EL GRECO   c. 1609 Oil
The Metropolitan Museum of Art, New York

EL GRECO'S life, of which so many of the facts are still unknown, interests us insofar as it explains his work. However, in this respect the little we know is precisely that which is essential. The work is very voluminous, though doubtless a considerable part of it has been lost. But in a country of hidden treasures such as Spain, there is reason to hope that this loss is only temporary—a hope that is the stronger in view of the relatively recent appreciation of the artist's work by the general public.

The extraordinary character, in the real sense of the word, of El Greco's work is largely explained by the known facts of the painter's origin. What has reached us concerning his life suggests the beauty of light and shade. There are deep shadows which torment the erudite not a little; there are flashes of light which dazzle the timid. The shadows are of unequal depth; they are full of color; they are not limited to bringing out the full drama of contrast but possess several degrees of revelation. But the essential remains the lights which these shadows bring out.

Only in recent years have we had reason to believe that El Greco was born in the tiny village of Fódele, situated in a Cretan valley a little to the west of Candia. His very surname Greco tells much—more than the name Domenico Theotocopuli, which we can ignore without loss and which in itself would merely indicate a Greek origin—even if a distant one. Spain has consecrated the name of Greco, which is Italian for the "Greek." Thus we learn that the artist whom Spain adopted really came from a Greek country, but after having sojourned in Italy.

Moreover, we already know from his own period that the Greece of this Greco was Crete, because he has at times added to his signature the

THE FAMILY OF EL GRECO OR OF HIS SON   Last period   Oil   39-2/5″ x 69⅔″
Collection Theodore Pitcairn, Bryn Athyn, Pa.

word "Cretan." His friend Fray Hortensio Felix Paravicino—of whom he has left two portraits, and who has written four precious sonnets to the painter—recalls in two instances his Cretan origin. But we have even more precise information: Giulio Clovio, who was his protector in Rome, commended him to Cardinal Alessandro Farnese as "A young native of Candia, a pupil of Titian." Lastly, a document of the Tribunal of the Inquisition at Toledo, dated May, 1582, indicates that the painter served as interpreter in connection with a lawsuit of one of his compatriots. From all this it is evident that El Greco stayed long enough in his first country to assimilate its culture. The inventory of his library further shows that he read Greek with predilection.

Fódele is situated between sheer cliffs close by the sea and is surrounded by pine and olive trees whose perfume and silvery foliage El Greco was to find again in Toledo. In that small village certain traditions were bound to be better preserved than they could be in a capital exposed to contacts with the outside world. Which icons, statues, and paint-

ings in the church of Fódele imprinted on the soul of the young Domenikos his first idea of beauty? What decorated ceramics or popular images formed the child's vision? This is a theme which offers an endless source for individual speculation. We know how pervasive art was in everyday life in Greek countries. We know that Crete was the center of one of the richest civilizations of antiquity; and also that, artistically, it was the most modern. Not only painting, sculpture, and architecture, but the art-industries of carving, metalwork, ceramics, and marquetry had all been known in Crete since the second millennium before our era.

But if Crete was favorable to the hatching of artistic genius, it provided small outlet for a painter conscious of the value of his work. Domenico went to Venice because it exerted a double attraction as both the metropolis for his small island and also as one of the world centers of painting. And in that fabulous city he was inevitably drawn to the one painter who epitomized its art:

[6]

*ST. MARTIN AND
THE BEGGAR* 1597-99
Oil 76⅛" x 40½"
*National Gallery of Art,
Washington, D.C.,
Widener Collection*

ST. FRANCIS IN MEDITATION   1604-14   Oil   66½" x 40⅝"
National Gallery of Canada, Ottawa

Titian. Beyond doubt, El Greco's technical competence dates from this visit—that virtuoso technique which renders superfluous the apologies of those persons who are shocked by the artist's boldness. El Greco thus became Titian's pupil, confounding future critics who find a greater affinity between his works and those of Tintoretto than those of his master.

Somewhat later, in Rome, El Greco learned to appreciate Michelangelo, an influence which also left its traces despite the fact that, at a much later date, he was to refer to the master of the Sistine ceiling as "a good fellow, but he didn't know how to paint." In Rome, at all events, Domenico's technical apprenticeship was completed. Thus Italy was responsible for the exterior, the material, the least personal side of his art. Here, too, he completed the portrait of his friend Giulio Clovio. Yet the glory of Rome suited him no better than the obscurity of Fódele. To judge from his work of this period, he sensed the profound antagonism that divided the Italians of the Renaissance, on the one hand ungovernable, pagan, pleasure-seeking, on the other austere, discreet, capable of loving aestheticism and appreciating mysticism.

So El Greco left Italy. His name next appears in a document dated 1577 in Toledo—where he was to die. By the time of his death he had been in the city for nearly forty years—more than half of his lifetime, more than three-quarters of his span as a

ST. FRANCIS IN MEDITATION
Detail of page 30

creative artist. Why he came to Spain we do not know. When questioned in connection with a lawsuit in which he was involved, he refused to state his reasons for this move. Possibly the offers which Charles V had made to Titian had something to do with it; or the fact that this monarch's son, since 1575, had been pushing the work of the Escorial—a great center of attraction for artists and builders of the day.

While the rich heritage of Crete and the consummate skill of Italy all played a role in the formation of this painter, the peninsula of the Tagus offered him a revelation. If we know nothing of the human friendships of El Greco, nothing of his human loves, we at least see how much he loved Toledo. Even today we can understand his reasons for this, for Time, perhaps in the artist's honor, has suspended its flight over the city. Nothing that makes its beauty today was missing at the period when El Greco lived there. Of the monuments, nothing essential to his vision is gone excepting

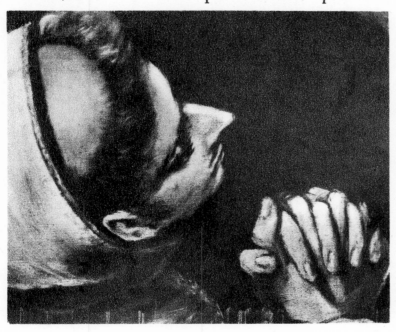

ST. FRANCIS IN MEDITATION
Detail of page 8

CHRIST BEARING THE CROSS   Oil   20⅞″ x 14-9/10″
Art Gallery, Athens

CHRIST ON THE CROSS WITH TWO WORSHIPPERS

c. 1580   Oil   102″ x 66″   *Louvre Museum, Paris*

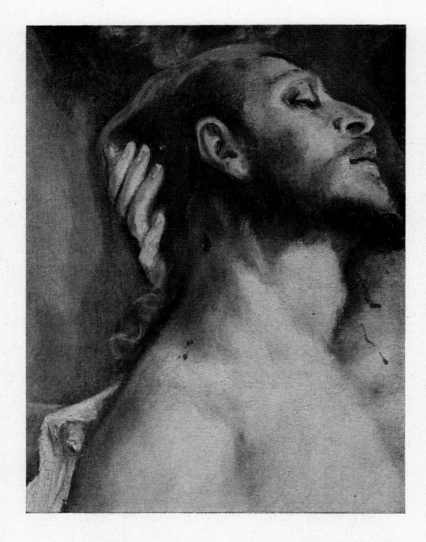

PIETA   Detail of page 64

alone the Alcazar, devoured, as it were, by the stormy sky against which he painted it.

Today as then, the silence of Toledo covers an intense spiritual life. Here St. Theresa had laid the foundations of a great religious house. It was in Toledo that Cervantes not only set the scene but subsequently produced *La Illustre Fregona,* published with the other *Novelas exemplares in 1613.* Great writers of the Church had worked here, including an illustrious Jesuit who compiled the life of St. Ignatius Loyola. From the portrait that El Greco painted of Diego Covarrubias it can be assumed that he knew the latter's brother, a great Hellenist and lawyer who played an important role in the Council of Trent.

El Greco lived at Toledo in a house, or rather a group of houses, which belonged to the Marqués de Villena near the synagogue, on the present Paseo del Tránsito. There exist some interesting documents relating to this dwelling. The Mar-

qués de Villena was suspected of magic, and his houses were built upon the foundations of the house of one Samuel Levy, who was the trusted confidant of Pedro I, but who was finally dispossessed by the king and so tortured that he died. In popular imagination the vast subterranean passages of this house were filled with treasure (and this is not counting the ones which El Greco created there, for it was in this dwelling that he painted, among others, the *Burial of Count Orgaz.* In any case, the memories of the rich Jewish treasurer and the magician marquis accord well with the mysterious character of the painter. Today, those apartments which he rented have disappeared with the decayed houses of which they once were a part. Situated in front of what is now called the "House of El Greco," they were thus nearer to the Tagus which raises among the grey rocks its tumultuous roar as it rushes in its downward course to join the Vega.

Here El Greco installed himself on a grand scale. He probably occupied the larger part of the Marqués de Villena's houses, for we find that he paid (because of his enlarged premises) from 596 to 1,200 reales for his privileges, while the neighboring tenants paid at the maximum 300 and for the most part 59 to 100 reales. Such grandeur was the result of important commissions of relatively early date. Soon after his arrival in Toledo, El Greco received an order for important work for the Convent of Santo Domingo el Antiguo, and, a little later, the Chapter of the Cathedral ordered from him an *Espolio.*

This latter work gave rise to a lawsuit the details of which are most instructive. The Chapter and the painter were not in agreement concerning the value of the work, nor on the suitability of certain details which the clergy judged insufficiently orthodox. Though El Greco obstinately refused to change anything, he eventually accepted a price lower than the one asked. An arbitration of the case, dated June 23, 1579, concluded that, though the value of the work "in proportion to the merits of its rich composition" doubtless deserved a remuneration in excess of the current prices of the day, the artist would have to "content himself with 3,500 reales." At this rate the young and relatively unknown painter received the equivalent of three years' occupancy of the large apartments of the Marqués de Villena.

Another testimony presents some exact details on this matter of the fortune and luxurious tastes of El Greco. The nineteenth century writer Jusepe Martínez—a little scandalized—tells us that he earned an abundance of ducats but that he spent them in ostentatious luxury, and to such a point that he hired musicians who played while he took his meals so that he might enjoy all pleasures simultaneously. With this, however, went an ill-spread board for, as in his painting, he was singular in all things. And indeed, the inventory of his possessions at the time of his death again does not seem to accord with the magnificence of a man who rented twenty-four rooms from the Marqués de Villena.

We are forced to conclude that this space served primarily to house his paintings. Martínez again informs us that at his death he left as his sole wealth two hundred canvases. The inventory gives exact figures: one hundred and forty-three paintings, ten large, thirty-seven small, ten very small. The remainder are unspecified. A second inventory made by the artist's son Jorge Manuel on April 12, 1614, mentions two hundred and forty-one pictures. Although the bulk of them were finished, Cossio, writing in 1908, adds that there are hardly more than twenty-five of these works to be found at that time in the catalogue of El Greco's output. A splendid prospect for those who hope to discover lost masterpieces! It therefore seems clearly indicated that El Greco painted largely for himself. Those two hundred and forty-one canvases were evidently not orders because, had they been so, he would not have had to contemplate the sale of his possessions.

This same inventory gives us additional interesting details regarding El Greco's books. His library comprised twenty-seven Greek works, the titles of which are given, headed by the Bible and Homer. St. Basil and St. John Crysostom, Demosthenes and Isocrates, Aesop and Lucian likewise figure there, as does Euripides. The library also contained sixty-seven Italian volumes and seventeen in Spanish. Although the titles of the last mentioned are not listed, there is good reason to believe that El Greco was in touch with, if not

THE VIRGIN
1594-97   Oil   20½" x 14¼" *Strasbourg Museum*

actually influenced by, the Golden Age of Spanish literature.

Eight days before his death, El Greco dictated his last will and testament. "Being," he said, "stretched upon my bed, suffering a malady which it has pleased the Lord to send me . . . and having treated . . . with Jorge Manuel Theotocoupli my son and Doña Jerónima de las Cuebas, who is a person of trust and good conscience . . . I confer full powers on my aforesaid son." Thus Jorge Manuel was entrusted with the carrying out of all legacies, religious or otherwise. El Greco followed this by naming Jorge Manuel "who is my son and that of the said Doña Jerónima de las Cuebas" as the inheritor of all his possessions. The will, dated March 31, 1614, was signed before witnesses with an illegible signature bearing hardly any resemblance to the magnificent one which appears on several of his paintings.

Of affiliated interest is the fact that El Greco has left us a document of a quality rare in the history of the art of his period: a painting representative of family life—a family which under the circumstances could hardly have been other than his own. For, at that period, no one thought of ordering from a painter a picture of intimate household doings. Rich and important people had themselves painted in ceremonial dress, more or less in costumes which recalled their social activities. This particular canvas consequently presents a wide field for guesswork. As the artist had no daughter, the young woman in the center of the picture could only have been his daughter-in-law, Alfonsa de los Morales. The child, which a servant on the right is holding, may be the eldest of El

THE ANNUNCIATION
Oil   50-2/5" x 32-3/5"
Collection Ralph M. Coe, Cleveland

It has been pointed out that in this will Jorge Manuel is not specified as a *legitimate* son, any more than Doña Jerónima is qualified as the painter's wife. At the same time it is altogether probable that this foreign artist, crowned with prestige and commissions, might have settled down shortly after his arrival in Toledo. The fact of his marriage to a Toledan would explain why he installed himself permanently in a city which had ceased to be the capital. Doña Jerónima gave birth to Jorge Manuel in 1578. In 1614 El Greco, in his will, honored her as a person of confidence and good conscience. The homage of the dying man who had just affirmed his fidelity to the Church has definite value. Furthermore, it may be noted in general that the Spanish wife, much more than the French or the English woman, retains her personality and her name.

CHRIST ON THE MOUNT OF OLIVES
Oil   29½" x 18½"
Collection Count A. Contini-Bonacossi, Florence

THE RESURRECTION
1595-1603
Oil   108" x 50"
Prado, Madrid

ST. JEROME PENITENT   1596-99   Oil   40-1/6" x 37-2/5"
                        National Gallery of Scotland, Edinburgh

Greco's grandchildren, born in 1604. The young woman who is spinning and the one holding the child are evidently servants—those family retainers who, the records tell us, remained in the artist's household for decades. One may conjecture

whether one of them did not serve as the painter's model for the *Veronica* in the San Vicente Museum in Toledo. As for the old woman, she may well have been the model for the St. Anne who appears in the painting of the *Holy Family* in the

ST. JEROME PENITENT   Detail of page 16

ANGELS' CONCERT upper part of ANNUNCIATION   Last period   Oil   45¼" x 85-2/5"
Art Gallery, Athens

Prado. Her features are noble and regular. Her finely pleated headdress, though designed for indoor wear, has the majesty of a judge's wig. Is this Catalina, mother of El Greco's daughter-in-law, or the woman whom he loved long and faithfully?

Not even the consolation of breaking into his tomb—as into that of a Pharaoh—is ours. He was buried, in accordance with his wish, in the church of the Community of Santo Domingo el Antiguo, but the remains were eventually transferred to San Torcuato by Jorge Manuel. In so doing, the latter requested a repository for his own family and for his *parents*—words that seem to strengthen the claim of El Greco's marriage to Doña Jerónima de las Cuebas.

San Torcuato has been swept away. Even in the immobility of death El Greco escapes us. We must be content to know him spiritually. Have we even an idea of what his features were like? It has been surmised that we can identify him in the personage who figures with Titian, Michelangelo, and Giulio Clovio in the lower right hand corner of Minneapolis' *Christ Driving Out the Money Changers;* and again in the centurion who appears in two versions of the *Espolio.* Aureliano de Beruete,

[18]

an astute connoisseur who has done much toward reinstating El Greco in his true position as a great artist, believes that he can recognize the painter in the very beautiful portrait in his own possession— that of a man on the threshold of old age, a man with a very extensive forehead, a pointed beard intersecting his ruff, and that penetrating, haunting gaze which is, nevertheless, veiled by inattention to the exterior world. We find this figure again in the *Martyrdom of St. Maurice* and in the *Burial of Count Orgaz,* directing his piercing look at the spectator as though inviting him to fully understand the lesson that emanates from the scene. Others believe that, following a frequent usage of the day, El Greco rendered himself in the person of St. Luke, patron of artists.

Several periods can be distinguished in El Greco's work. Deprived as we are of his Cretan products, we are obliged to begin with his Italian period when the example of Titian, Tintoretto, and Michelangelo acted as an incentive toward technical perfection. It took Spain to release El Greco from the Italian yoke. Within this liberated period of the artist's life we can distinguish two phases. In the first he regained his indepen-

THE LAOCOON   1606-10   Oil   54" x 67⅞"

National Gallery of Art, Washington, D.C., Kress Collection

dence. In the second he gradually enclosed himself within the world he had created, building upon certain singularities, eventually to crystallize his childlike simplicity into the simplicity of an old man. The artist did not live long enough to produce those works which the artist alone can "see"; though there is plenty of controversial material in his later paintings, of whose figures Barrès writes, "Before our very eyes we see them attain spirituality. The magic of enthusiasm pierces and transfigures them."

Rather than raise at this point the merits of his last manner, we would prefer to discuss that providential moment in his creation in the contemplation of which all of his admirers can meet and find

themselves in agreement. It was the moment when El Greco painted the *Burial of Count Orgaz*. He was then in the full maturity of his forty-five years. It is easy to show that the subject must have pleased him. Among other things, it was said that Count Orgaz was descended from Don Pedro Paleologue, third son of the Emperor of Constantinople. Thus the Iberianized Greek glorified another Greek, longer if not more strongly Iberianized.

On March 18, 1586, a contract was drawn up and signed between the painter and the Vicar of Santo Tomé. This document related to obtaining authorization from the Archbishop to execute a picture. Said picture "was to be painted in the

[19]

CHRIST DRIVING THE MONEY-CHANGERS FROM THE TEMPLE 1571-76 Oil 46″ x 59″
The Minneapolis Institute of Arts

Chapel of the Immaculate Conception, from the top of the arch . . . to the epitaph which is on the wall, and the canvas must represent how, in the following of people amongst whom the Vicar and the other ecclesiastics proceeded to the ceremonies of the interment of Don Gonzalo Ruiz of Toledo, Lord of the Villa de Orgaz, Saint Augustin and Saint Stephen descended to inter the body of this gentleman, one taking him by the head and the other by the feet and placing him in the tomb. There must be shown around this scene a number of people looking on, and above all the glory of the open sky.''

These involved specifications in no way dismayed the artist. On the contrary, they served to

exalt and stimulate his genius. In sober and subtle terms the Vicar of Santo Tomé and the divines of the archbishopric defined the work as a masterpiece.

Though representing a funeral, there is nothing sad about the *Burial of Count Orgaz*. The figures are, of course, in mourning, but the feeling that they express is profound joy at the moment when a miracle gives them the certainty that their friend is welcomed in the sky. This joy is grave in the presence of two great saints and is also accompanied by humility, for the certainty of their friend's salvation does not guarantee their own. Thus, as in his *Saint Maurice,* El Greco introduced the supernatural within the frame of the natural

CHRIST BEARING THE CROSS   1578-80   Oil   25" x 20½"
Courtesy Tomas Harris, Ltd., London

THE VISITATION   1604-14   Oil   38⅛" x 28⅛"

Library and Collection, Harvard University
Courtesy of the Dumbarton Oaks Research

[22]

PORTRAIT OF GIULIO CLOVIO, THE MINIATURE PAINTER
1571-73   Oil   25½" x 37-2/5"
National Museum, Naples

without diminishing any of its grandeur. At the service of so sublime a conception the painter has placed his prodigious technical virtuosity. One can be sure that the distortions in it were entirely intentional. For to heighten its spiritual power, El Greco has modified his drawing, projecting his figures heavenwards and translating with surprising foreshortenings and violent torsions the vehemence of feeling which the impassive faces may not betray.

The color, on the other hand, is modified toward reality. In Rome, and above all in Venice, El Greco had learned all the mysteries, the enchantment, of color. But Spain, where the landscape is so often monochrome—and monochrome without gradations—taught him a more profound and ascetic plane of reality. His palette reduced itself to five colors: white, ivory black, vermilion, yellow ochre, and rose madder. Especially in his portraits of men the monochrome character of the Spanish countryside is recalled. Even his Cardinals, subjects which generally demand such intensity of coloring, are little removed from the portraits of gentlemen in black coats. A certain contemporary writer has hailed Velasquez as the old master who first introduced that modern color—grey—in painting. Yet this tribute could more justly be made to El Greco. He it was, and no other, who initiated this new era, the discoverer of the New World of the palette. The austerity and truth in color ordinarily practiced by Velasquez are in accordance with the lesson of El Greco, whom he admired and deeply understood.

El Greco was an architect and a sculptor as well as a painter. We know that he worked in the former capacity at the Cigarral de Buenavista, a country estate where Cardinal Sandoval y Rojas liked to entertain the distinguished men of his day. From this practice, however limited, he came to understand that a painting is not sufficient unto itself but that it must have a determined destination and place in a building. Its exact adaptation to its situation is among the elements of perfection in the *Burial of Count Orgaz*.

As a sculptor the artist has left us few works. The most interesting one is a high relief which

ST. JAMES THE GREAT
1599-1601 Oil 27½" x 21¼"
Formerly Collection S. Del Monte, Brussels

represents the Virgin giving a chasuble to Saint Ildefonso. Formerly in the Toledo Cathedral, this example, for all its beauty, has a somewhat rough appearance, or, if you like, is related to the primitive—a manner which should not be confused with the disciplined violence of his painting. It may be that the material El Greco used, which was wood, had something to do with this. But if not greatly significant in themselves, such sculptural works, like his architectural experience, served the painter well. El Greco sought in sculpture a further means of attaining the truth. In addition to wood, he used more supple materials, modeling either in clay or in wax the preparatory figures for his compositions. The contemporary painter and critic Francisco Pacheco tells in 1611 of having seen in his home a cupboard filled with these statuettes. Through them El Greco studied scrupu-

lously the play of shadow and light and the stability of the figures themselves, sometimes pushing his experiments to the furthest limits, yet never losing his respect for the real.

Pacheco throws in another piece of valuable information as regards El Greco's working methods. At the request of the aged painter, Jorge Manuel showed Pacheco a large hall in which there were to be found, in small scale, "the originals of everything that he had painted in his lifetime." In what way did these preliminary studies serve El Greco? This again, we feel, was his method of keeping in touch with reality. He believed (and this is a very old Eastern conception) that the spiritual powers, when represented in human form, must be larger than common humanity. In an inscription relating to *Saint Ildefonso* the painter tells us that he wanted to make the figures large "since they were celestial figures and that lights, even small, seem large when seen from afar." "To be dwarfed is the worst thing that can befall any kind of figure" run the words in a legal document relating to one of the numerous lawsuits which El Greco had to plead on the subject of his paintings—a statement which successfully refutes the alleged deficiencies of vision of this prodigious seer.

Suffice it to say that El Greco disconcerts us in the same way that we are disconcerted by the *Cante Jondo*—a national Spanish music form derived in part from the Byzantine chant of the early Church, in part from the Arab invaders, and lastly, influenced by the gypsy immigration. Not unlike the primitive chant of the East, the *Cante Jondo* is built on a finer division of intervals than exists in our musical scale. Its melodic curve is not scanned by measure, while "the use of a single note is reiterated to obsession and very often accompanied by . . . ornamental adjunctions . . . like the expansions or flights of feeling suggested by the emotive force of the text."

THE VIRGIN WITH SANTA INES
AND SANTA TECLA
1597-99 Oil 76⅛" x 40½"
National Gallery of Art, Washington, D.C.,
Widener Collection

ST. LOUIS OF FRANCE
(*or St. Ferdinand of Castile*)
Detail of page 37

This repetition of a single note to the point of obsession is extremely significant in connection with the work of El Greco, of whom it has been said "His whole life is centered on the same idea." Among his known works there are at a minimum ten pictures of the *Adoration of the Shepherds,* eight of the *Holy Family,* sixty-seven of *St. Francis,* and twelve of *Christ Bearing the Cross.* These series of works represent the *Cante Jondo* of painting—the Eastern and Spanish expression, in brief, the Catholic, which stands for the most profound of religious sentiments.

Shall we say that El Greco was a mystic? The mystic states are those in which a human being communicates directly with his creator independent of the official way which the Church opens to the Christian collectivity. This communication cannot be other than strictly personal and mysterious; and the painting which presents to us images which are valid to all spectators thus stops on the

threshold of the mystic. But it is possible that El Greco felt such interior impulses that he sought to cross that threshold; and it is there that the majority of mortals can no longer follow him. If Spanish mysticism has had its painter, it is he who, years after the death of the model, by the grace of the spirit, gave such vigorous form to the mortal features of Juan de Avila.

Glory has been for El Greco as the Kingdom of Heaven, which is conquered by violence. Singular from its origin, his destiny remains singular beyond the tomb. Many have divined and felt his genius rather than undersood it. Moreover, he ends by imposing himself, without a single concession, upon the general public. At times his work reflects the sacred grandeur of Byzantine design; at times, more superficially, he reflects the Italian Renaissance. He is too Spanish not occasionally to communicate a romantic emotion: he has his nocturnes and his "desired storms." In certain color passages we can find an invitation to Impressionism. At other times one may detect a fugitive Cubist tendency to present an object seen from many sides within the same moment of time. This artist, who possessed every aptitude, used his liberty of choice authoritatively. Unlike his contemporaries, he never amused himself by painting still-life, nor did he treat landscape for its own sake (his Toledo is, like the city itself, essentially a person). Many of his paintings are not only outside the limits of time but beyond the range of space—pictorially a prodigious accomplishment.

Among painters, Velasquez was the first who understood El Greco. It was he who chose some of his paintings for the royal collections, at the same time reserving one or two for himself. But above all, Velasquez transmitted the message of El Greco with so much persuasive power that he induced his contemporaries to forget the over-violent role of the precursor. How can we insist upon finding "sad" in El Greco's work the very atmosphere which Velasquez loved? Certainly, contrary to ancient mythology, for which shadow was of the other world, and light of this world, in El Greco's Catholic conception, it was this world which was dark, but only so in relation to that world "where the real sun lights other skies," and toward which religion and sanctity open up for us perspectives already inundated with a joyous light. El Greco established a communication more or less broad according to the circumstances, but permanent, between this world, which is never desolate, and the beyond.

El Greco's latter-day protagonists have essentially been men of vision. "About 1890," wrote the critic Arsène Alexandre, "there were quite ten of us in Paris who liked the works of this painter. Théodore Duret had seen and appreciated them on the spot, and he had offered one to the Louvre, which accepted it with no great enthusiasm. Degas owned one of his paintings which had been in the possession of J. F. Millet. Ignacio Zuloaga was making his debut as a painter . . . and as a messenger of El Greco's work wherever he could. Yet everyone turned a deaf ear . . . At that time I was able to convince myself, at Toledo itself, of the forgetfulness and disdain in which the Spaniards themselves held poor Theotocopuli." The prestige

associated with these distinguished names, together with the study bestowed on the artist by the eminent scholar Maurice Barrès, marked the beginning of the El Greco revival and inevitably resulted in the discovery of a fairly large number of El Grecos, some of doubtful authorship.

As a synthesis of a national culture, the great Spanish painter, Zurbaran, so deeply representative of the religious spirit of Spain, will appear to some more Spanish than El Greco. This will doubtless be because the latter's intense Spanish sense was part of a prodigious universality. It might, however, be well to transpose the question and ask ourselves which is the more Spanish of the two Spains: the one which fiercely shuts itself up in its *castillo interior,* or the one whose civilization shone forth on the world and constituted the greatest and most lasting of empires? Seen in this light we can recognize that, spiritually, Zurbarán was a monk and El Greco a "Conquistador."

MAURICE LEGENDRE

ST. ILDEFONSO   c. 1605   Oil   44¼″ x 25¾″
National Gallery of Art, Washington, D.C., Mellon Collection

PORTRAIT OF THE ARCHITECT DON ANTONIO COVARRUBIAS
1601-09   Oil   26¾″ x 22″
Museum of El Greco, Toledo

THE ESPOLIO, THE THREE MARYS   Detail of page 31

THE ESPOLIO   1583-84   Oil   64-9/10″ x 39″
Old Pinakothek, Munich

ST. VERONICA WITH THE SUDARIUM   1590-95   Oil
Formerly Vogel, Weisbaden

[32]

THE HOLY FAMILY   Detail of page 35

THE HOLY FAMILY Detail of page 35

THE HOLY FAMILY WITH BOWL OF FRUIT   1592-96   Oil   51-1/5″ x 39-2/5″
Courtesy The Cleveland Museum of Art

[35]

ST. LOUIS OF FRANCE (or St. Ferdinand of Castile)
Detail of page 37

ST. LOUIS OF FRANCE (or *St. Ferdinand of Castile*)   1586-90   Oil   46″ x 37-2/5″
Louvre Museum, Paris

BURIAL OF COUNT ORGAZ   1586   Oil   15′ 9″ x 11′ 8″

Church of Santo Tomé, Toledo

BURIAL OF COUNT ORGAZ

Detail of page 38

BURIAL OF COUNT ORGAZ

Detail of page 38

[40]

BURIAL OF COUNT ORGAZ   Detail of page 38

[41]

BURIAL OF COUNT ORGAZ

Detail of page 38

[42]

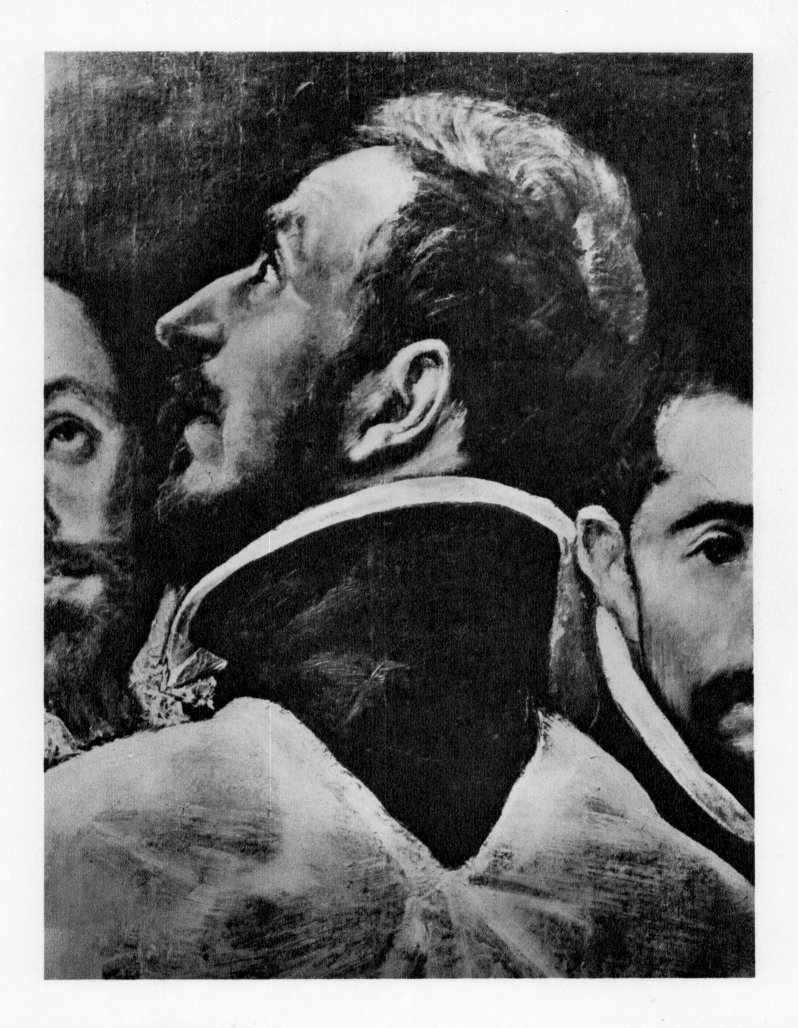

BURIAL OF COUNT ORGAZ

Detail of page 38

[43]

CHRIST DRIVING THE MONEY-CHANGERS FROM THE TEMPLE
after 1604   Oil   41-1/3" x 50"
National Gallery, London

CHRIST DRIVING THE MONEY-CHANGERS FROM THE TEMPLE
Detail of page 44

TOLEDO IN A STORM   Last period   Oil   47¾″ x 42¾″
The Metropolitan Museum of Art, New York

ST. JOHN THE BAPTIST AND ST. JOHN THE EVANGELIST
1595-1604   Oil   42-9/10" x 33½"
Hospital of S. Juan Bautista, Toledo

**ST. ANNE, THE VIRGIN AND THE INFANT CHRIST WITH
ST. JOHN, HOLDING A BOWL OF FRUIT**

1592-97   Oil   63" x 39-2/5"   *Museum of San Vicente, Toledo*

PORTRAIT OF A YOUNG WOMAN WITH A FUR   c. 1577   Oil
Collection Sir John Stirling-Maxwell, Pollok House, Glasgow

ST. JEROME   1584-94 Oil 43⅜" x 37½"

Copyright The Frick Collection, New York

ST. FRANCIS

Collection Rolfe de Maré, Paris

Oil   26-1/6" x 21"

THE PENITENT ST. PETER   1596-1600 Oil 48¼" x 40¼"

Fine Arts Gallery of San Diego

[52]

ST. JAMES THE LESS   1603-12   Oil   39" x 31-1/10"

Museum of El Greco, Toledo

ST. THOMAS   1603-12   Oil   39" x 31-1/10"

Museum of El Greco, Toledo

[54]

ST. JAMES THE GREAT   1603-12   Oil   39" x 31-1/10"

Museum of El Greco, Toledo

ST. BARTHOLEMEW

Museum of El Greco, Toledo

1603-12   Oil   39" x 31-1/10"

[56]

ST. FRANCIS IN ECSTASY

Detroit Institute of Arts

1585-90 Oil

[57]

ST. JOHN THE EVANGELIST   1603-12   Oil   39" x 31-1/10"

               Museum of El Greco, Toledo

[58]

ST. PAUL   1603-12   Oil   39" x 31-1/10"

Museum of El Greco, Toledo

ST. MATTHEW

Museum of El Greco, Toledo

1603-12 Oil 39" x 31-1/10"

[60]

ST. DOMINICK IN PRAYER 1588-91   Oil   46½″ x 33⅞″
Collection A. Sans Bremon, Valencia

ST. PHILIP   1603-12   Oil   39" x 31-1/10"

Museum of El Greco, Toledo

CARDINAL NINO DE GUEVARA   1596-1600   Oil   67¼″ x 42¼″
The Metropolitan Museum of Art, New York

PIETA   1592-95 Oil 47¼″ x 57″   *Collection Comtesse de la Béraudière, Paris*

[64]

ST. ANDREW

1603-12 Oil

Museum of El Greco, Toledo

ST. SIMON

1603-12   Oil   39" x 31-1/10"

Museum of El Greco, Toledo

ST. LUKE   after 1600   Oil   24-9/10″ x 21″
Courtesy The Hispanic Society of America, New York

THE MAGDALENE

Worcester Art Museum

1577-80 Oil 42" x 40"

[68]

BIBLIOGRAPHY

ABBOTT, JERE. "The Geometry of the Art of El Greco," in Art Studios, 1927, v. 5, pp. 91-96, ill., 2 plates.

ALEXANDRE, ARSENE. Histoire de l'art décoratif du XVIe siècle à nos jours.
Paris, H. Laurens, 1892.

AYALA, JERONIMO LOPEZ CEDILLO, CONTE DE. De la religiosidad y del misticismo en las obras del Greco. Madrid, 1915.

BARRES, MAURICE. Greco, ou le secret de Tolède. 13. éd. Paris, Emile-Paul, 1912. Nouv. éd. 1923.

BARRES, MAURICE et LAFOND, PAUL. Le Greco. Paris, H. Floury, 1931.

BERITENS, DR. GERMAN. Aberraciones del Greco cientificamente consideradas. Madrid, 1913.
— El Astigmatismo del Greco. Madrid, 1914.

BERTAUX, EMILE. "Commentaire du livre de San Román," in Revue de l'art ancien et moderne, June 1911. Paris.

BERUETE Y MORET, A. DE. El Greco, pintor de retratos. Toledo. 1914; Madrid, Blass y Ca., 1914.

BIKELAS, DEMETRIUS. La Grèce byzantine et moderne: essais historiques. Paris, F. Didot et Cie, 1893.
— Etude sur Greco. Athens, 1894.

BORJA DE SAN ROMAN Y FERNANDEZ, FRANCISCO DE. El Greco en Toledo; ó, Nuevas investigaciones acerca de la vida y obras de Domenico Theotocópulos. Madrid, V. Suárez, 1910.
— El sepulcro de los Theotocópulos. Madrid, 1912.
— "De la vida del Greco. Nueva series de documentos inéditos," in Archivo español de arte y arqueología, nos. 8-9, 1927.

BUSUIOCEANU, ALEXANDRU. "Les Tableaux du Greco dans la collection royale de Roumanie," in Gazette des Beaux-Arts, May 1934, Paris.

BYRON, ROBERT, and RICE, TALBOT. The Birth of Western painting. London, G. Routledge, 1930, with 94 plates.

BYRON, ROBERT. "Greco; the Epilogue to Byzantine Culture," in Burlington Magazine, v. 55, 1929, pp. 160-167. 5 plates.

CALVERT, ALBERT, and HARTLEY, C. GASQUOINE (pseud.) El Greco. London & New York, J. Lane Co., 1909.

CEAN-BERMUDEZ, JUAN AUGUSTIN. Diccionario histórico de los más ilustres profesores de las bellas artes en España. Madrid, Viuda de Ibarra, 1800.

COSSIO, MANUEL BARTOLOME. Lo Que se sabe de la vida del Greco. Madrid, Clásica, 1913, 1914.
— El Greco; with 193 plates. 2 vols. Madrid, V. Suárez, 1908.

DOMENECH GALLISSA, RAFAEL. La Casa del Greco. Barcelona, Hijos de J. Thomas, 1914.

DURAND, PAUL. Manuel d'iconographie chrétienne grecque et latine, tr. du manuscript byzantin "Le Guide de la peinture," avec une introduction et des notes par Adolphe Napoléon Didron. Paris, Imprimerie royale, 1845.

ESCHOLIER, RAYMOND. Greco. "Anciens et modernes." No. 13. Paris, Floury, 1937.

ESPRESATI, CARLOS G. La Casa del Greco. Madrid, 1912.

FIGUERAS PACHECO, FRANCISCO. Arte de la pintura. Seville, 1649.

GESSNER, ADOLF. Die Spanier, El Greco, Velasquez, Goya. Berlin, Gustav Weise, 1939.

GOLDSCHEIDER, LUDWIG. El Greco; London, George Allen & Unwin, Ltd., 1938. Ill.

GOLDSCHMIDT, ADOLF. "Grecos Augenkrankheit," in Süddeutsche Monatshefts. Munich, 1911.

GOMEZ DE LA SERNA, RAMON. El Greco, el visionario de la pintura. Santiago de Chile, Ediciones Ercilla, 1941. (Colleccion contemporaneos.)

GRISWOLD, F. G. El Greco, Ltd. ed. New York, Duttons, Inc., 1930.

GUINARD, PAUL. Madrid; l'Escorial et les anciennes résidences royales. Paris, H. Laurens, 1935.

HEINEMANN. Catalogue de l'exposition espagnole. Munich, 1911.

JORGE, RICARDO. "El Greco," in Revista de universidade de Coimbra (Portugal), 1912.

JUSTI, CARL. Diego Velasquez und sein Jahrhundert. Bonne, 1881.
— El Greco, in Zeitschrift für bildende Kunst. Leipzig, 1897.
— El Greco. Vollständige aufl. Zürich, Phaidon-Verlag, c1933.

KEHRER, HUGO. Die Kunst des Greco. Munich, Hugo Schmidt, 1914.

LACOSTE, J. Catálogo illustrado de los obras de Domenico Theotocópulos. Madrid, 1902.

LAFOND, PAUL. Le Greco, essai sur sa vie, ses oeuvres. Paris, 1913.

LAMBERT, ELIE. "Les procédés du Greco," in Gazette des Beaux-Arts, Paris, 1921.
— Tolède. Paris, 1925.

LEGENDRE, MAURICE, and HARTMANN, A. Domenikos Theotokopoulos called El Greco. The Commodore Press, London. 1937.

LOSTALOT DE BACHOUET, ALFRED. Etude dans les musées de Madrid. Paris, 1895.

MADRAZO Y KUNTZ, PEDRO DE. Catalogue du Prado. Madrid, 1904.

MARTINEZ, JOSE. Discursos practicables del nobilisimo arte de la pintura. Madrid, La Real Academia de San Fernando, 1886.

MARTINI, PIETRO. Del pittore Domenico Teotocopulo e di suo dipinto. Torino, 1866.

MARTYNE, CHARLES. "Notice biographique sur El Greco," in E. Bénézit. Dictionnaire des peintres, dessinateurs et graveurs, tome III. Paris, 1924.

MAUCLAIR, CAMILLE. Le Greco. Paris, 1931.

MAYER, AUGUST LIEBMANN. Eine Einführung in das Leben und Werken des Domenico Theotocopulos, genannt El Greco. Munich, Delphin-Verlag, 1911, 1912.
— Il Greco. (Biblioteca d'arte illustrata, Serie I, Fasc. 8.) Rome, 1921.
— El Greco, kritisches und illustriertes Verzeichnis des Gesamtwerkes. Munich, F. Hanfstaengl, 1926.
— El Greco. Berlin, Klinkhardt & Biermann, 1931.
— "El Greco, an Oriental artist," in The Art Bulletin, v. 11, pp. 146-152, June 1929.

MEIER-GRAEFE, JULIUS A. Die spanische Reise. Berlin, S. Fischer, 1910.
— The Spanish Journey, tr. by J. Holroyd-Reece, with drawings by J. Sima, and 9 plates after paintings by El Greco. London, Jonathan Cape, 1926.

MILIZIA, FRANCESCO. Dizionario delle belle arti del disegno. 2 vols. Bassano, 1797.
— Ibid. Ed. corretta . . . Bologna, Stamperia Cardinali e Frulli, 1827.

MORALEDA Y ESTEBAN, JUAN. Dos Grecos más en Toledo. Toledo, 1910.

MADRID. MUSEO DEL PRADO. Catalogo. 1933.

NAGLER, GEORG KASPAR. Künstler-Lexicon, v. XVIII. Munich, 1848.

PALOMINO de CASTRO Y VELASCO, DON ANTONIO. El Museo Pictórico y Escala Optica. 3 vols. Madrid, 1724; 1795-97.
— Histoire abrégée des plus fameux peintres. Paris, 1749.

PONZ, DON ANTONIO. Viage de España, en que se dá noticia de las cosas más apreciables y dignas de saberse que hay en ella . . . Madrid, Jachin Ibarra, 1776.

ROSENKRANZ, HANS. El Greco and Cervantes: Two Men in Revolt; tr. by Marcel Aurousseau. New York, Davies, 1932.
— Ibid., with title: El Greco and Cervantes in the Rhythm of Experience. London, Davies, 1932.

SANTOS, PADRE FRANCOIS DE LOS. Descripcion de Real monasterio de San Lorenzo del Escorial. Madrid, Impr. Bernardo de Villa Diego, 1681.

SCHEPPELER, Oberst. Beiträge zur spanischen Kunstgeschichte. Aix-la Chapelle, 1828.

SIERRA CORELLA, ANTONIO. "Le Musée S. Vicente de Tolède," in Mouseion, Bulletin de l'Office international des musées, September 1929.

STEINBART, KURT. "Greco und die Spanische Mystik," in Repertorium für Kunstwissenschaft, Berlín, v. 36, p. 121 ff.

SYMONS, ARTHUR. "Domenico Theotocopuli. A Study at Toledo, 1899," in Cities and Seacoasts and Islands. London, Collins, 1918.

TORMO, ELIAS. "La Patrie natale du Greco," in El Debate, Feb. 8, 1935.

TRAPIER, ELIZABETH DU GUE. "El Greco," in Hispanic Notes and Monographs; Peninsular Series. New York, 1925.

UNAMUNO Y JUGO, MIGUEL DE. "Etude sur Greco, à l'occasion du troisième centenaire de sa mort," in Rassegna del arte, Rome, 1914, v. 14, pp. 75-85, ill.

UTRILLO, MIQUEL. El Greco. Barcelona. 1906.

VIARDOT, LOUIS. Notices sur les principaux peintres de l'Espagne. Paris, 1839.

VILLAR, EMILIO H. DEL. El Greco en España. Madrid, 1928.

VINIEGRA, SALVADOR. Catalogo illustrado de la exposición de los obras de Domenico Theotocopulos llamado El Greco. Madrid, 1902.

WILLUMSEN, JENS FERDINAND. La Jeunesse du peintre El Greco; essai sur la transformation de l'artiste byzantin en peintre européen. 2 vols. Paris, G. Crès & Cie., 1927.

INDEX OF ILLUSTRATIONS

Color Plates are listed in italics